SHAPE WALK

Written by Anita Parks
Photographs by Justin Kirchoff

ScottForesman

A Division of HarperCollins*Publishers*

We're going for a walk.

We see circles.

We see rectangles.

We see diamonds.

We see triangles.

We see squares.

What shapes can you see?